Computerised Accounting Practice Set Using Reckon Accounts

Entry Level

This entry level computerised accounting practice set is for students who need to practice exercises of Reckon Accounts software, students can record a month's transactions of Mobiles 4 U Pty Ltd and can create financial reports.

It covers the following topics.

- Setting Up a New Accounting System
- Suppliers, Purchases and Inventory
- Customers, Sales and Inventory
- Receipts, Payments and Expenses
- Bank Reconciliation
- Financial Reports

ESSTEE BOOKS

Syed Tirmizi
Certified Advisor

ISBN 978-0-9945988-8-2

9 780994 598882 >

Part A
Practice Set

This page is blank.

Instructions

You have been appointed as an Accounts Assistant at Mobiles 4 U Pty Ltd, a new company dealing in smartphones. The company started trading on 1ˢᵗ April 2016.

You are required to create company data file in Reckon Accounts, process business transactions and produce financial reports for the month of April 2016.

Create a Company File

Setup Interview	
Company Name	Mobiles 4 U Pty Ltd
Tax ID	ACN 111 222 333
Address	23 Spring Street
City	Melbourne
State and Post Code	VIC 3000
Industry	Product Sales/Retail
Business Entity	Company Tax Return
Financial Year Starts	July
Services or Products	Products only
Track Tax	Yes
Use Sales Receipts	Yes
Use Billing Statements	Yes
Use Invoices	Yes
Keep Track of Bills	Yes
Track Inventory	Yes
Employees	Yes
Date to Start Tracking	01-04-2016
Add Bank Account	Yes
Bank Account Details	Mobiles 4 U Pty Ltd – 987654321, Opened on 01-04-2016

Record Business Transactions

(Purchases, Sales, Inventory, Receipts, Payments and Expenses)

1ˢᵗ April   Paul Edwards made a deposit of $25,000 by cheque # 000982 into the Cheque Account as start-up capital for the business.

4ᵗʰ April   Bill received from Office Business Supplies amount $2,250 (including tax) for the following expenses.

Supplier Details	
Supplier Name	Office Business Supplies
Address	23 Spring Street
City	Melbourne
State and Post Code	VIC 3000
Terms	Net 15
Tax Code	NCG
Ref. No.	OBS7659
Memo	Office Business Supplies

Account	Tax	Gross	Memo
Office Supplies	NCG	$750	Stationery
Office equipment	NCG	$1,000	Computer & Printer
Furniture and Fittings	NCG	$500	Desk & Chair
Tax	☑ Amounts include tax		

4th April Office Business Supplies bill # OBS7659 paid by Cheque No. 1.

6th April 200 Voice V10 Smartphones purchased from Speedy Communications Pty Ltd at $95 each (including tax).

Supplier Details	
Supplier Name	Speedy Communications Pty Ltd
Address	14 Abbott Street,
City	Melbourne
State and Post Code	VIC 3000
Terms	1 % 10 Net 30
Tax Code	NCG
Ref. No.	SC825
Memo	Speedy Communications Pty Ltd
Item Details	
Item Information	
Type	Inventory Part
Item Name/Number	V10
Purchase Information	
Description	Voice V10 Smartphone
Gross Cost	$95 per each
Tax Code	NCG
COGS Account	Cost of Goods Sold
Sales Information	
Description	Voice V10 Smartphone
Gross Amt.	$145 per each
Tax Code	GST
Income Account	Sales
Tax	☑ Amounts include tax

9th April Paid $19,000 by Cheque No. 2 for the Smartphones purchased on 6th April.

11th April Wireless Telecommunications Pty Ltd purchased 100 Voice V10 Smartphones. An Invoice issued for 100 Voice V10 Smartphones at $145 including tax. Invoice No. 1.

Customer Details	
Customer Name	Wireless Telecommunications Pty Ltd
Address	41 High Street
City	Melbourne
State and Post Code	VIC 3000
Terms	Net 15
Tax Code	GST
Tax	☑ Amounts include tax

18th April   Sold further 50 Voice V10 Smartphones to Wireless Telecommunications Pty Ltd at $145 each includes tax. The Invoice No. is 2.

19th April   Cheque # 000149 received from Wireless Telecommunications Pty Ltd amount $14,500 for the settlement of the Invoice No. 1. Cheque deposited to the Cheque Account on the same day.

23rd April   Wireless Telecommunications Pty Ltd returned 10 Voice V10 Smartphones. Issue a Credit Note and apply credit to the Invoice No. 2. Credit No. 3.

26th April   Electricity bill received. Process the transaction as memorised transaction.

Supplier Details	
Supplier Name	Victoria Electricity
Address	P. O. Box 99
City	Melbourne
State and Post Code	VIC 3000
Terms	Due on receipt
Tax Code	NCG
Ref. No.	0215393
Amount	$200 include tax. (Use Electricity Account)
Memo	Victoria Electricity
Memorised Transaction	
Type	Remind Me
How Often	Monthly
Next Date	26/05/2016

26th April   Paid $200 by Cheque No. 3 to Victoria Electricity.

Reconcile Bank Account

30th April   Prepare bank reconciliation for the month of April 2016. Process following bank charges before starting bank reconciliation, details are as follows.

Cheque No.	BS
Amount	$10
Memo	Bank charges
Account	Account Keeping Fee
Tax	NCF

Further details can be obtained from the statement on the next page.

BANK OF RICHMOND

36 Spring Street, Richmond, VIC 3121
TEL 1800 AUSTRALIA

Cheque Account Statement
30/04/2016

Mobiles 4 U Pty Ltd
45 Bay Road
Melbourne
VIC 3000

BSB Number	Account Number
123 456	987654321

Date	Details	Ref	Withdrawals	Deposits	Balance
01-Apr-16	Account opened - Initial deposit			$25,000.00	$25,000.00
05-Apr-16	CHQ 0001		$2,250.00		$22,750.00
10-Apr-16	CHQ 0002		$19,000.00		$3,750.00
19-Apr-16	Cheque deposited			$14,500.00	$18,250.00
30-Apr-16	Bank charges		$10.00		$18,240.00
	Totals		**$21,260.00**	**$39,500.00**	

Produce Financial Reports

30th April   Print or save the following reports for the month of April 2016.

   I.   Cheque Account Reconciliation
   II.   General Ledger Report (In Use)
   III. Customer Balance Detail
   IV.   Supplier Balance Detail
   V.   Memorised Transaction Listing
   VI.   Inventory Valuation Detail
   VII. Expenses by Supplier Detail
   VIII. Statement of Cash Flows
   IX.   Trial Balance
   X.   Profit and Loss Detail
   XI.   Balance Sheet

Part B
Solutions

This page is blank.

Mobiles 4 U Pty Ltd
Reconciliation Detail
Mobiles 4 U Pty Ltd, Period Ending 30-04-2016

Type	Date	Num	Name	Clr	Amount	Balance
Beginning Balance						0.00
Cleared Transactions						
Cheques and Payments - 3 items						
Bill Pmt -Cheque	04-Apr-2016	1	Office Business Supplies	X	-2,250.00	-2,250.00
Bill Pmt -Cheque	09-Apr-2016	2	Speedy Communications Pty Ltd	X	-19,000.00	-21,250.00
Cheque	30-Apr-2016	BS	Bank of Richmond	X	-10.00	-21,260.00
Total Cheques and Payments					-21,260.00	-21,260.00
Deposits and Credits - 2 items						
Deposit	01-Apr-2016			X	25,000.00	25,000.00
Deposit	19-Apr-2016			X	14,500.00	39,500.00
Total Deposits and Credits					39,500.00	39,500.00
Total Cleared Transactions					18,240.00	18,240.00
Cleared Balance					18,240.00	18,240.00
Uncleared Transactions						
Cheques and Payments - 1 item						
Cheque	26-Apr-2016	3	Victoria Electricity		-200.00	-200.00
Total Cheques and Payments					-200.00	-200.00
Total Uncleared Transactions					-200.00	-200.00
Register Balance as of 30-04-2016					18,040.00	18,040.00
Ending Balance					**18,040.00**	**18,040.00**

Mobiles 4 U Pty Ltd
General Ledger
As of April 30, 2016

Accrual Basis

Type	Date	Num	Name	Amount	Balance
Mobiles 4 U Pty Ltd					0.00
Deposit	01-Apr-2016			25,000.00	25,000.00
Bill Pmt -Cheque	04-Apr-2016	1	Office Business Supplies	-2,250.00	22,750.00
Bill Pmt -Cheque	09-Apr-2016	2	Speedy Communications Pty Ltd	-19,000.00	3,750.00
Deposit	19-Apr-2016			14,500.00	18,250.00
Cheque	26-Apr-2016	3	Victoria Electricity	-200.00	18,050.00
Cheque	30-Apr-2016	BS	Bank of Richmond	-10.00	18,040.00
Total Mobiles 4 U Pty Ltd				18,040.00	18,040.00
Trade receivables					0.00
Tax Invoice	11-Apr-2016	1	Wireless Telecommunications Pty Ltd	14,500.00	14,500.00
Tax Invoice	18-Apr-2016	2	Wireless Telecommunications Pty Ltd	7,250.00	21,750.00
Payment	19-Apr-2016	000149	Wireless Telecommunications Pty Ltd	-14,500.00	7,250.00
Adjustment Note	23-Apr-2016	3	Wireless Telecommunications Pty Ltd	-1,450.00	5,800.00
Total Trade receivables				5,800.00	5,800.00
Inventory Asset					0.00
Bill	06-Apr-2016	SC825	Speedy Communications Pty Ltd	17,272.73	17,272.73
Tax Invoice	11-Apr-2016	1	Wireless Telecommunications Pty Ltd	-8,636.37	8,636.36
Tax Invoice	18-Apr-2016	2	Wireless Telecommunications Pty Ltd	-4,318.18	4,318.18
Adjustment Note	23-Apr-2016	3	Wireless Telecommunications Pty Ltd	863.64	5,181.82
Total Inventory Asset				5,181.82	5,181.82
Undeposited Funds					0.00
Payment	19-Apr-2016	000149	Wireless Telecommunications Pty Ltd	14,500.00	14,500.00
Deposit	19-Apr-2016		Wireless Telecommunications Pty Ltd	-14,500.00	0.00
Total Undeposited Funds				0.00	0.00
Furniture and Fittings					0.00
Bill	04-Apr-2016	OBS7659	Office Business Supplies	454.55	454.55
Total Furniture and Fittings				454.55	454.55
Office furniture/equipment					0.00
Bill	04-Apr-2016	OBS7659	Office Business Supplies	909.09	909.09
Total Office furniture/equipment				909.09	909.09
Trade creditors					0.00
Bill	04-Apr-2016	OBS7659	Office Business Supplies	-2,250.00	-2,250.00
Bill Pmt -Cheque	04-Apr-2016	1	Office Business Supplies	2,250.00	0.00
Bill	06-Apr-2016	SC825	Speedy Communications Pty Ltd	-19,000.00	-19,000.00
Bill Pmt -Cheque	09-Apr-2016	2	Speedy Communications Pty Ltd	19,000.00	0.00
Total Trade creditors				0.00	0.00
Tax Payable					0.00
Bill	04-Apr-2016	OBS7659	Australian Taxation Office	204.54	204.54
Bill	06-Apr-2016	SC825	Australian Taxation Office	1,727.27	1,931.81
Tax Invoice	11-Apr-2016	1	Australian Taxation Office	-1,318.18	613.63
Tax Invoice	18-Apr-2016	2	Australian Taxation Office	-659.09	-45.46
Adjustment Note	23-Apr-2016	3	Australian Taxation Office	131.82	86.36
Cheque	26-Apr-2016	3	Australian Taxation Office	18.18	104.54
Cheque	30-Apr-2016	BS	Australian Taxation Office	0.00	104.54
Total Tax Payable				104.54	104.54
Owner's Equity					0.00
Deposit	01-Apr-2016		Paul Edwards	-25,000.00	-25,000.00
Total Owner's Equity				-25,000.00	-25,000.00
Sales					0.00
Tax Invoice	11-Apr-2016	1	Wireless Telecommunications Pty Ltd	-13,181.82	-13,181.82
Tax Invoice	18-Apr-2016	2	Wireless Telecommunications Pty Ltd	-6,590.91	-19,772.73
Adjustment Note	23-Apr-2016	3	Wireless Telecommunications Pty Ltd	1,318.18	-18,454.55
Total Sales				-18,454.55	-18,454.55
Cost of Goods Sold					0.00
Tax Invoice	11-Apr-2016	1	Wireless Telecommunications Pty Ltd	8,636.37	8,636.37
Tax Invoice	18-Apr-2016	2	Wireless Telecommunications Pty Ltd	4,318.18	12,954.55
Adjustment Note	23-Apr-2016	3	Wireless Telecommunications Pty Ltd	-863.64	12,090.91
Total Cost of Goods Sold				12,090.91	12,090.91
Bank Charges					0.00
Cheque	30-Apr-2016	BS	Bank of Richmond	10.00	10.00
Total Bank Charges				10.00	10.00

Page 1

Mobiles 4 U Pty Ltd
General Ledger
As of April 30, 2016

Accrual Basis

Type	Date	Num	Name	Amount	Balance
Electricity					0.00
Cheque	26-Apr-2016	3	Victoria Electricity	181.82	181.82
Total Electricity				181.82	181.82
Supplies					0.00
Office					0.00
Bill	04-Apr-2016	OBS7659	Office Business Supplies	681.82	681.82
Total Office				681.82	681.82
Total Supplies				681.82	681.82
TOTAL				**0.00**	**0.00**

Mobiles 4 U Pty Ltd
Customer Balance Detail
All Transactions

Type	Date	Num	Account	Amount	Balance
Wireless Telecommunications Pty Ltd					
Tax Invoice	11-Apr-2016	1	Trade receivables	14,500.00	14,500.00
Tax Invoice	18-Apr-2016	2	Trade receivables	7,250.00	21,750.00
Payment	19-Apr-2016	000149	Trade receivables	-14,500.00	7,250.00
Adjustment Note	23-Apr-2016	3	Trade receivables	-1,450.00	5,800.00
Total Wireless Telecommunications Pty Ltd				5,800.00	5,800.00
TOTAL				**5,800.00**	**5,800.00**

Mobiles 4 U Pty Ltd
Supplier Balance Detail
All Transactions

Type	Date	Num	Account	Amount	Balance
Office Business Supplies					
Bill	04-Apr-2016	OBS7659	Trade creditors	2,250.00	2,250.00
Bill Pmt -Cheque	04-Apr-2016	1	Trade creditors	-2,250.00	0.00
Total Office Business Supplies				0.00	0.00
Speedy Communications Pty Ltd					
Bill	06-Apr-2016	SC825	Trade creditors	19,000.00	19,000.00
Bill Pmt -Cheque	09-Apr-2016	2	Trade creditors	-19,000.00	0.00
Total Speedy Communications Pty Ltd				0.00	0.00
TOTAL				**0.00**	**0.00**

Mobiles 4 U Pty Ltd
Memorised Transaction Listing
April 30, 2016

Transaction	Type	Source Account	Amount	Frequency	Auto	Next Date
Victoria Electricity	Cheque	Mobiles 4 U Pty Ltd	-200.00	Monthly	No	26-May-2016

Page 1

Mobiles 4 U Pty Ltd
Inventory Valuation Detail
April 2016

Type	Date	Name	Num	Qty	Cost	On Hand	Avg Cost	Asset Value
Inventory								
Voice V10 Smartphones								
Bill	06-Apr-2016	Speedy Communications Pty Ltd	SC825	200	17,272.73	200	86.36	17,272.73
Tax Invoice	11-Apr-2016	Wireless Telecommunications Pty Ltd	1	-100		100	86.36	8,636.36
Tax Invoice	18-Apr-2016	Wireless Telecommunications Pty Ltd	2	-50		50	86.36	4,318.18
Adjustment Note	23-Apr-2016	Wireless Telecommunications Pty Ltd	3	10		60	86.36	5,181.82
Total Voice V10 Smartphones						60.00		5,181.82
Total Inventory						60.00		5,181.82
TOTAL						**60.00**		**5,181.82**

Mobiles 4 U Pty Ltd
Expenses by Supplier Detail

Accrual Basis

April 2016

Type	Date	Num	Account	Clr	Amount	Balance
Office Business Supplies						
Bill	04-Apr-2016	OBS7659	Office		681.82	681.82
Total Office Business Supplies					681.82	681.82
Victoria Electricity						
Cheque	26-Apr-2016	3	Electricity		181.82	181.82
Total Victoria Electricity					181.82	181.82
TOTAL					**863.64**	**863.64**

Mobiles 4 U Pty Ltd
Statement of Cash Flows
April 2016

	Apr 16
OPERATING ACTIVITIES	
Net Income	5.490.00
Adjustments to reconcile Net Income	
to net cash provided by operations:	
Trade receivables	-5,800.00
Inventory Asset	-5,181.82
Tax Payable	-104.54
Net cash provided by Operating Activities	-5,596.36
INVESTING ACTIVITIES	
Furniture and Fittings	-454.55
Office furniture/equipment	-909.09
Net cash provided by Investing Activities	-1,363.64
FINANCING ACTIVITIES	
Owner's Equity	25,000.00
Net cash provided by Financing Activities	25,000.00
Net cash increase for period	18,040.00
Cash at end of period	**18,040.00**

Mobiles 4 U Pty Ltd
Trial Balance

Accrual Basis

As of April 30, 2016

	Apr 30, 16	
	Debit	Credit
Mobiles 4 U Pty Ltd	18,040.00	
Trade receivables	5,800.00	
Inventory Asset	5,181.82	
Undeposited Funds	0.00	
Furniture and Fittings	454.55	
Office furniture/equipment	909.09	
Trade creditors	0.00	
Tax Payable	104.54	
Owner's Equity		25,000.00
Sales		18,454.55
Cost of Goods Sold	12,090.91	
Bank Charges	10.00	
Electricity	181.82	
Supplies:Office	681.82	
TOTAL	**43,454.55**	**43,454.55**

Page 1

Mobiles 4 U Pty Ltd
Profit & Loss Detail
Accrual Basis   April 2016

Type	Date	Num	Name	Clr	Amount	Balance
Ordinary Income/Expense						
Income						
Sales						
Tax Invoice	11-Apr-2016	1	Wireless Telecommunications Pty Ltd		13,181.82	13,181.82
Tax Invoice	18-Apr-2016	2	Wireless Telecommunications Pty Ltd		6,590.91	19,772.73
Adjustment Note	23-Apr-2016	3	Wireless Telecommunications Pty Ltd		-1,318.18	18,454.55
Total Sales					18,454.55	18,454.55
Total Income					18,454.55	18,454.55
Cost of Goods Sold						
Cost of Goods Sold						
Tax Invoice	11-Apr-2016	1	Wireless Telecommunications Pty Ltd		8,636.37	8,636.37
Tax Invoice	18-Apr-2016	2	Wireless Telecommunications Pty Ltd		4,318.18	12,954.55
Adjustment Note	23-Apr-2016	3	Wireless Telecommunications Pty Ltd		-863.64	12,090.91
Total Cost of Goods Sold					12,090.91	12,090.91
Total COGS					12,090.91	12,090.91
Gross Profit					6,363.64	6,363.64
Expense						
Bank Charges						
Cheque	30-Apr-2016	BS	Bank of Richmond		10.00	10.00
Total Bank Charges					10.00	10.00
Electricity						
Cheque	26-Apr-2016	3	Victoria Electricity		181.82	181.82
Total Electricity					181.82	181.82
Supplies						
Office						
Bill	04-Apr-2016	OBS7659	Office Business Supplies		681.82	681.82
Total Office					681.82	681.82
Total Supplies					681.82	681.82
Total Expense					873.64	873.64
Net Ordinary Income					5,490.00	5,490.00
Net Income					**5,490.00**	**5,490.00**

Page 1

Mobiles 4 U Pty Ltd
Balance Sheet
As of April 30, 2016

Accrual Basis

	Apr 30, 16
ASSETS	
Current Assets	
Chequing/Savings	
Mobiles 4 U Pty Ltd	18,040.00
Total Chequing/Savings	18,040.00
Accounts Receivable	
Trade receivables	5,800.00
Total Accounts Receivable	5,800.00
Other Current Assets	
Inventory Asset	5,181.82
Total Other Current Assets	5,181.82
Total Current Assets	29,021.82
Fixed Assets	
Furniture and Fittings	454.55
Office furniture/equipment	909.09
Total Fixed Assets	1,363.64
TOTAL ASSETS	**30,385.46**
LIABILITIES	
Current Liabilities	
Other Current Liabilities	
Tax Payable	-104.54
Total Other Current Liabilities	-104.54
Total Current Liabilities	-104.54
TOTAL LIABILITIES	**-104.54**
NET ASSETS	**30,490.00**
EQUITY	
Owner's Equity	25,000.00
Net Income	5,490.00
TOTAL EQUITY	**30,490.00**

Page 1

www.ingramcontent.com/pod-product-compliance
Lightning Source LLC
Chambersburg PA
CBHW060515060326
40689CB00020B/4757